W9-CDH-484

Harley-Davidson

By John Hamilton

VISIT US AT
WWW.ABDOPUBLISHING.COM

Published by ABDO Publishing Company, PO Box 398166, Minneapolis, MN 55439.
Copyright ©2014 by Abdo Consulting Group, Inc. International copyrights reserved
in all countries. No part of this book may be reproduced in any form without written
permission from the publisher. A&D Xtreme™ is a trademark and logo of
ABDO Publishing Company.

Printed in the United States of America, North Mankato, Minnesota.
112013
012014

 PRINTED ON RECYCLED PAPER

Editor: Sue Hamilton
Graphic Design: Sue Hamilton
Cover Design: John Hamilton
Cover Photo: Glow Images
Interior Photos: All photos Harley-Davidson Motor Company except: AP-pgs 1 & 2-3;
Corbis-pgs 8, 9, 13, 14-15, 30-31 & 32.

ABDO Booklinks
Web sites about motorcycles are featured on our Book Links pages. These links are
routinely monitored and updated to provide the most current information available.
Web site: www.abdopublishing.com

Library of Congress Control Number: 2013946164

Cataloging-in-Publication Data

Hamilton, John, 1959-
  Harley-Davidson / John Hamilton.
    p. cm. -- (Xtreme motorcycles)
Includes index.
ISBN 978-1-62403-220-2
1. Harley-Davidson motorcycle--Juvenile literature.   2. Motorcycles--Juvenile
literature.   I. Title.

Contents

The Harley-Davidson Appeal

There's something unforgettable about a Harley. For more than 110 years, Harley-Davidson has made motorcycles that work hard, impress, and thrill.

Harley-Davidsons have an unmistakable rumble as they cruise down the road. These American classics represent freedom, individuality, and adventure.

Company History

Harley-Davidson was founded in 1903. Four friends from Milwaukee, Wisconsin, began building motorcycles in a wooden shed. The young men included William S. Harley and brothers Arthur, Walter, and William Davidson.

Arthur Davidson   Walter Davidson   William Harley   William Davidson

Their motorcycles had a reputation for being tough and reliable. By 1919, the company was producing more than 23,000 bikes per year. Government contracts during World War I and World War II boosted production even more.

After World War II, Harley-Davidson kept growing and changing. The company became famous for its heavyweight cruiser motorcycles. Loyal customers were attracted to the Harley brand by new engine designs and the use of color and styling.

Custom 1940s Harley-Davidson Knucklehead

In the 1960s and 1970s, the company faced stiff competition

from Japanese and British motorcycle companies. By the late 1980s, Harley-Davidson reestablished itself. Its headquarters remains in Milwaukee, Wisconsin. The company sells hundreds of thousands of bikes each year worldwide.

1960 Harley-Davidson FLH Duo-Glide

XTREME FACT – Because of its famous logo, Harley-Davidson is often referred to as "the bar and shield."

V-Twin Engine

Harley-Davidson motorcycles are famous for their V-Twin engines.

Early in the company's history, bikes were made with a single-cylinder engine. To produce more power, Harley-Davidson added an extra cylinder. It was joined to the crankshaft and case at a 45-degree angle to form a "V" shape. The design was modified and refined over the years, but the rumbling "big twin" engine remains a Harley hallmark.

Two workers at a Harley-Davidson assembly plant attach a V-Twin engine to a motorcycle's frame.

Racing

By 1911, many other companies were making motorcycles. But Harley-Davidson bikes were preferred by many racers. The company started an official racing department in 1914. Harley-Davidson-supported bikers won so many races they became known as the Wrecking Crew.

Harley-Davidson first created a racing team in 1914. The racers and bikes soon ruled the sport.

Today, the Harley racing tradition continues with the Screamin' Eagle/Vance & Hines NHRA Pro Stock Motorcycle team. These drag racers have won many NHRA world championships riding Harley bikes.

Andrew Hines makes a warm-up run down a track before a NHRA race.

Harley Culture

Harley-Davidson riders are loyal customers. There's something about riding a Harley that makes them feel like part of a large family. There are Harley clubs and riders' groups all over the world.

MOTOR HARLEY-DAVIDSON CYCLES

Harley-Davidson owners gather in Sturgis, South Dakota, for the annual motorcycle rally.

Rallies at such places as Sturgis, South Dakota, and Daytona Beach, Florida, attract thousands of Harley riders each year. Despite their "outlaw" reputation, Harley owners come from all walks of life. They find common ground in the road, the wind, and the bikes they ride.

Sportster

The Sportster line was introduced in 1957. It is the longest-running Harley-Davidson family of bikes still in production. Originally intended as racers, Sportsters evolved into lean, high-spirited street machines.

Sportsters use powerful 883 or 1,200 cc Evolution V-Twin engines. They have narrow frames and low seats. Agile handling makes them fun to ride on any twisty road.

2014 Sportster XL 883 SuperLow

17

Dyna

The Dyna line includes the Wide Glide, Super Glide, Fat Bob, and Switchback models. They are Harley-Davidson's performance leaders of bikes equipped with "big twin" engines. Dating back to 1971, Dynas have traditional cruiser styling. The front end resembles the Sportster model, but it is combined with a unique, rigid frame and a big engine. Rubber engine mounts reduce vibration. Dynas are relatively lightweight and have excellent road handling. Many Dyna owners customize their bikes.

FXDWG Dyna Wide Glide

Dyna FXDF Fat Bob

Softail

Harley-Davidson Softail bikes use big twin engines and traditional cruiser styling. They are called Softail because they hide rear-wheel suspension under the transmission. So even though they look like classic "hardtail" bikes, they have a very smooth ride. Softail bikes come in several models and custom styling.

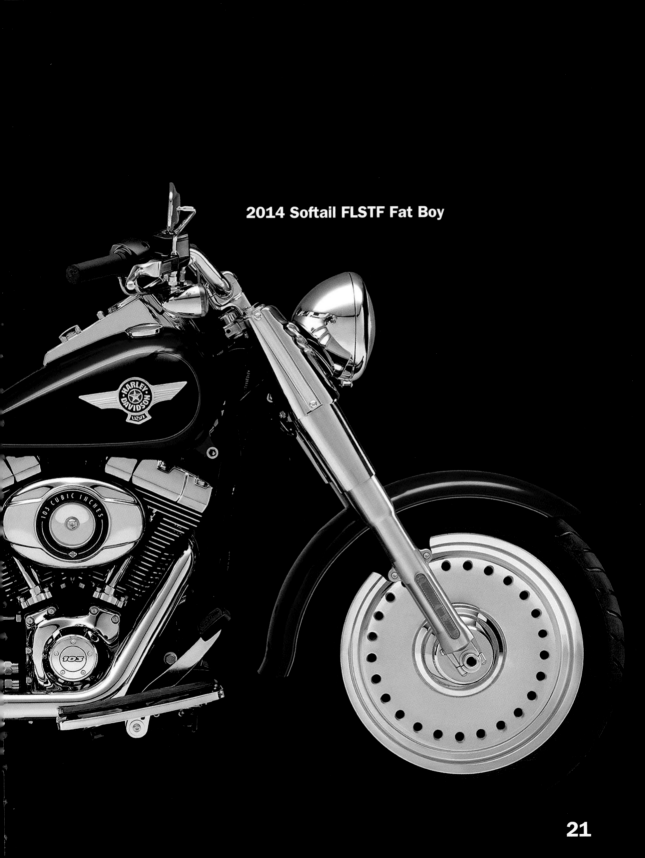

2014 Softail FLSTF Fat Boy

V-Rod

V-Rod motorcycles are a break from Harley-Davidson tradition. They use a Revolution V-Twin engine, which was developed jointly with German auto manufacturer Porsche.

2014 VRSCDX Night Rod Special

Unlike other Harley big twin engines, the Revolution is a 60-degree V-Twin that uses overhead cams and liquid cooling. It produces tremendous power. These "power cruisers" are street bikes inspired by Harley-Davidson drag racing motorcycles.

Touring

Touring bikes are made for traveling long distances in comfort. They are also known as "dressers." Harley-Davidson Touring bikes have large windshields, powerful V-Twin engines, stiff fames, and plenty of luggage space in hard-sided saddlebags. Many Touring models also have great sound systems for playing favorite tunes on the open road.

XTREME FACT—In the 1920s, a group of farm boys with a hog mascot won races on Harley motorcycles. That is why the bikes are nicknamed "hogs."

Touring 2014 FLHTK
Electra Glide Ultra Limited

Trike

Harley-Davidson Trike motorcycles have two wheels in back. They are for riders of all skill levels.

2014 FLHTCUTG Tri Glide Ultra Classic

Trike motorcycles are especially good for people who ride only occasionally but still love the feel of the open road on their faces. Trikes also appeal to riders who are physically challenged, or those worried about balance. Trikes have many of the same comfort features as Harley-Davidson Touring bikes. They are great machines for taking on long road trips.

CVO

CVO stands for Custom Vehicle Operations. Harley-Davidson CVO bikes are custom-built, limited-edition models based on existing Harley stock motorcycles.

2014 FXSBSE CVO Breakout

Each year, Harley chooses from its mass-produced stock bikes and gives them premium upgrades such as larger engines and custom paint jobs. They also can include electronic accessories such as radios and GPS navigation systems. Harley CVO bikes are special editions that always make a great first impression.

Glossary

CC (Cubic Centimeters)

Engines are often compared by measuring the amount of space (displacement) inside the cylinders where gas and air mix and are ignited to produce power. Displacement is measured in cubic centimeters.

Cruiser

A type of motorcycle where the rider sits in a laid-back posture with arms and feet forward. The Harley-Davidson company is known for its cruiser motorcycles.

Hardtail

Cycles built with a rigid, one-piece motorcycle frame and without rear suspension. The look is more streamlined, but the rider feels the bumps in the road.

NHRA

The National Hot Rod Association is the first national drag racing organization. It was formed in 1951 by enthusiast Wally Parks.

Porsche

A German company known for producing high-performance sports cars and custom motorcycles.

Pro Stock

A drag racing class where the racers are built with steel tubing and aerodynamic bodywork that resembles the motorcycles' street versions. They can run a quarter-mile (.4 km) course under seven seconds, at speeds of more than 195 miles per hour (314 kph).

Index